Catholic Women's Bible Study & Journal

The Littlest Way

SIRACH: CATHOLIC WOMEN>S BIBLE STUDY AND JOURNAL

©2016 The Littlest Way

ALL RIGHTS RESERVED

No part of this book may be reproduced in any form or by any electronic or mechanical means, including information storage and retrieval systems, without written permission form the author, except in the case of a reviewer, who may quote brief passages embodied in critical articles or in a review.

Scripture taken from The Holy Bible, Revised Standard Version, Catholic Edition

+J.M.J.+

I offer this humble work to the Mother of Jesus.

Remember, O most gracious Virgin Mary, that never was it known that anyone who fled to thy protection, implored thy help, or sought thine intercession was left unaided.

Inspired by this confidence, I fly unto thee, O Virgin of virgins, my mother; to thee do I come, before thee I stand, sinful and sorrowful. O Mother of the Word Incarnate, despise not my petitions, but in thy mercy hear and answer me.

Amen.

Mother's Day
May 8, 2016

Sirach:

Catholic Women's Bible Study and Journal

I believe any book that begins with the sentence, *"Wisdom comes from the Lord,"* needs to be read. And not only read, but studied and lingered over. How? Well, that is entirely up to you. You may feel called to journal through the Book of Sirach—old school, pen and paper style. You may be called to get your art on with the creative process of Bible journaling using various mediums from colored pencils, acrylic paints, washi tape and stickers. Or you may choose to dig deeper into the Book of Sirach by verse mapping your way through. Either way, this book will encourage you, help you and give you the room you need for whatever journaling style you choose.

First, a little history before we begin. The Book of Sirach is a teaching work written by the Jewish scribe Shimon ben Yeshua ben Eliezer ben Sira of Jerusalem, approximately 200 to 175 BCE. It is also called Book of Ecclesiasticus or the Wisdom of Sirach, not to be confused with the Book of Wisdom. The book itself is the largest wisdom book to have been preserved from antiquity. Sirach is accepted as part of the Christian biblical canon by Catholics, Eastern Orthodox, and most Oriental Orthodox and is cited or referred to frequently in the Epistle of James and by various Fathers of the Church. Although the Anglican Church does not consider it canonical, it encourages the reading of Sirach "for example of life and instruction of manners." The Lutheran Churches include it in their lectionaries, and as a book proper for reading, devotion, and prayer.

This Bible study and journal based on the Book of Sirach is meant to be used daily. But sometimes life throws us a curve ball or three. Keep at this study! If you miss a day or three, pick right back up where you left off. If a chapter a day is too much for you, break it up to suit your needs. The point is to read your Bible and make it your own.

This Bible study and journal is not deeply theological. It is not intended for you to earn a degree in Biblical Theology once completed. *It is intended* for your Bible to become a close companion, a regular on your nightstand, in your purse or on your kitchen counter. *It is intended* to deposit nuggets of the good, true and beautiful Word of God in your heart and mind to carry with you. *It is intended* to be profitable for teaching, for reproof, for correction, and for training in righteousness. (2 Timothy 3:16) Grab your Bible and any other necessary supplies and let's get started!

What is S.O.U.L?

Each day as we work through the Book of Sirach together, we will begin with a verse from that day's chapter, followed by a short reflection and maybe even a question. At the bottom of the page, there will be a quote from one of our beloved saints. The next page, the journaling page, well, this is all you!

As we journal our way through the Bible, we will be using the acronym **SOUL**.

Scripture....Observation....Understanding....Love

This acronym begins with **scripture.** I believe choosing one verse from a chapter being read and then writing it down is an important tool in Bible study. When we write something down, we assign importance to it. Think of things like appointments or birthdays; we write those down on a calendar or in our planner because we do not want to forget them. I believe we should do the same with the Word of God.

Next is **observation**. I look at this part of the acronym as the obvious: who is speaking, where are they, what are they doing...those kinds of questions.

Then, **understanding**. This is the fun part; this is the totally you part! What do you need to do to help you understand this passage better? I love looking up words in a Thesaurus! Finding synonyms helps me apply the verse to my season of life. Some women are artists and will be able to better understand a verse once they get out their art supplies and began painting or sketching. Hand lettering is a beautiful art form that pairs well with scripture. Still others find they are better able to grasp the meaning of a passage by "verse mapping." We each have our own ways of helping us better understand a passage. The journal pages in this book are wide open, giving your heart, mind and soul the necessary room to spread out and go deep into the Word of God.

Finally, **love**. This is where you spend time *with* Love. This may be handwritten prayers or poems to God. It may be intimate conversations you abbreviate or write long hand between you and the Lover of your soul. It might be blank space—mine typically is. *Let yourself go in this space.* It might be hard at first, this intimate silence, **keep trying.** This is where the brain disengages and it is all about the heart. Let me tell you again, *let yourself go.* You can trust Him. He will not hurt you, make fun of you or abandon you. He will only love you. All right, let's get started!

There is more information about Bible Journaling, Bible Study, Verse Mapping and studying the scriptures at

The Littlest Way

www.thelittlestway.com

Sirach 1

If you desire wisdom, keep the commandments, and the Lord will supply it for you.

Sirach 1:26

Do you know what wisdom means? Insight or common sense. This world could use a generation of people, Christians included and especially, who desire a good dose of common sense. Let's ask God for a *heavenly* dose of common sense. Let's keep the commandments (and if we do not know them we need to learn them), and then open our heart and mind to divine common sense, not worldly nonsense.

He who prays most receives most.

~ St. Alphonsus Maria de Liguori

Scripture Observation Understanding Love

Sirach 2

Accept whatever is brought upon you,

and in changes that humble you be patient.

Sirach 2:4

Verses 7, 8 and 9 have specific commands for those who fear the Lord. What are they?

As patience leads to peace, and study to science, so are humiliations the path that leads to humility.

~ St. Bernard of Clairvaux

Scripture Observation Understanding Love

Sirach 3

For great is the might of the Lord; he is glorified by the humble.

Sirach 3:20

In Matthew 11:29 our Lord instructs us to learn from Him for He is gentle and humble of heart. The reward for doing so is rest for our souls. How does the idea of rest strike you right now? Elusive? Sorely needed? A forgotten state of being?

Let's trust our Lord's words. Maybe instead of seeking rest, we should seek gentleness and humility *first* and that will lead to rest.

> "What will be the crown of those who, humble within and humiliated without, have imitated the humility of our Savior in all its fullness!
>
> ~ St. Bernardette

Scripture Observation Understanding Love

Sirach 4

Do not be reckless in your speech, or sluggish and remiss in your deeds.

Sirach 4:29

Do "reckless," "sluggish" or with "remiss" describe how we perform our daily duties? If we find ourselves performing our duties on autopilot, maybe we should begin them as St. Benedict instructs, with a prayer to our Lord asking Him to help us do them well.

"Whenever you begin any good work you should first of all make a most pressing appeal to Christ our Lord to bring it to perfection.

~ St. Benedict

Scripture Observation Understanding Love

Sirach 5

Do not follow your inclination and strength, walking according to the desires of your heart.

Sirach 5:2

Do you remember the popular phrase that made the rounds years ago, "What would Jesus do?" As commercialized as it became, it really does have some value. If we find ourselves being led by our emotions more than we would like, let's get into the practice of intentionally considering, "What *would* Jesus do?" And then do it.

*I will attempt day by day to break my will into pieces.
I want to do God's Holy Will, not my own!*

~ St. Gabriel of the Sorrowful Mother

Scripture Observation Understanding Love

Sirach 6

Whoever fears the Lord directs his friendship aright, for as he is, so is his neighbor also.

Sirach 6:17

When was the last time we considered our friendships? I mean seriously considered, "Is this relationship bringing me closer to God? Helping me to become the beautiful, wonderful, child of God He created me to be? Helping me to know, love and serve Him better?" If it has been a while...or never...maybe now is the time to put some serious thought into our friendships (in real life and on line).

Fly from bad companions as from the bite of a poisonous snake. If you keep good companions, I can assure you that you will one day rejoice with the blessed in Heaven; whereas if you keep with those who are bad, you will become bad yourself, and you will be in danger of losing your soul.

~ St. John Bosco

Scripture Observation Understanding Love

Sirach 7

In all you do, remember the end of your life, and then you will never sin.

Sirach 7:36

"Never sin??" Really? How is that even possible?

Have you ever read the admonition and instructions included at the bottom of this page? I found it in an old missal. The last line gives three specific instructions, what are they? Maybe those are the keys to not sinning?

> Remember, O Christian soul, That thou hast this day and every day of thy life...
>
> God to glorify, Jesus to imitate, A soul to save, A body to mortify, Sins to repent of, Virtues to acquire, Hell to avoid, Heaven to gain, Eternity to prepare for, Time to profit by, Neighbors to edify, The world to despise, Devils to combat, Passions to subdue, Death perhaps to suffer, Judgement to undergo.
>
> Therefore, O child of Jesus and Mary, Avoid sin and all its occasions. Pray often, go frequently to Confession and Holy Communion.

*S*cripture *O*bservation *U*nderstanding *L*ove

Sirach 8

Do not travel on the road with a foolhardy fellow, lest he be burdensome to you; for he will act as he pleases, and through his folly you will perish with him.

Sirach 8:15

So what exactly is a "foolhardy" fellow? Well, a couple of synonyms for "foolhardy" are: rash, imprudent, reckless, headstrong. Let me ask a question? How many of us have friends that are rash, imprudent, reckless or headstrong? Let me ask another question. How many of *us* are rash, imprudent, reckless or headstrong? Are we our own "foolhardy" fellow on the road of life? A burden to ourselves? Acting as we please?

The true servant of Jesus Christ bears all things; she labors much, and speaks little.

~ St. Mary Magdalen de Pazzi

Scripture Observation Understanding Love

Sirach 9

Do not envy the honors of a sinner, for you do not know what his end will be.

Sirach 9:11

Have we ever envied someone...until we got to know them? Usually once we get to know someone, we realize, *we all struggle with something.* Some of us just hide it better.

"We must often remember what Christ said, that not he who begins, but he that perseveres to the end, shall be saved.

~ St. Philip Neri

Scripture Observation Understanding Love

Sirach 10

*The beginning of man's pride is to depart from the Lord;
his heart has forsaken his Maker.*

Sirach 10:12

The beginning of our pride is not the fancy new car, lovely new shoes and matching purse or various accolades. *The beginning of our pride is the moment we shift our focus away from God, our Creator.* Honestly, it is not the car, shoes, purse, recognition…we can have all those and remain humble…*if we keep God as our focus.*

"You must ask God to give you power to fight against the sin of pride which is your greatest enemy – the root of all that is evil, and the failure of all that is good. For God resists the proud.

~ St. Vincent de Paul

Scripture Observation Understanding Love

Sirach 11

Good things and bad, life and death, poverty and wealth, come from the Lord.

Sirach 11:14

Are we in the habit of recognizing God only in the "good stuff" and wondering where He is in the "not so good stuff?"

One of the most intense periods of suffering in my life produced one of the most spiritually fruitful periods as well. Can you recall a period of the same?

As iron is fashioned by fire and on the anvil, so in the fire of suffering and under the weight of trials, our souls receive that form which our Lord desires them to have.

~ St. Madeline Sophie Barat

Scripture Observation Understanding Love

Sirach 12

*Who will pity a snake charmer bitten by a serpent,
or any who go near wild beasts?*

Sirach 12:13

Are there people, places or things that are occasions of sin for us physically, mentally or spiritually? We need to identify those occasions, confess the sins involved and then avoid them so we do not risk falling into the same sin over and over.

Speak a great deal with God, and little with men.

~ St. Ephrem

SCRIPTURE **O**BSERVATION **U**NDERSTANDING **L**OVE

Sirach 13

Keep words to yourself and be very watchful, for you are walking about with your own downfall.

Sirach 13:13

I do not know about you, but I did not need a scripture verse to tell me I am walking around with my own downfall. The thing is, if I would just stop and ask myself, "Are these words kind, true or necessary?" I would save myself **lots** of "talker's remorse."

A vain question deserves nothing but silence. So learn to be silent for a time; you will edify your brethren and silence will teach you to speak when the hour is come.

~ St. Vincent Ferrer

Scripture Observation Understanding Love

Sirach 14

*Do not deprive yourself of a happy day;
let not your share of desired good pass by you.*

Sirach 14:14

I love this verse! When I was in the process of retraining my mind to think *what I wanted it to think about* instead of anything that popped into it, this was one of the verses I repeated to myself daily. It reminded me, **I have a choice about how my day is going to go.** I can choose a happy day or I can choose to deny myself that joy. Life is going to happen, the good, bad and ugly. But I can choose how to respond to each of those instances.

*All the things that are now worrying you can be put
into a smile which shows your love of God.*

~ St. Josemaria Escriva

Scripture Observation Understanding Love

Sirach 15

*If you will, you can keep the commandments,
and to act faithfully is a matter of your own choice.*

Sirach 15:15

Here is another verse reminding us, **we have a choice in our life.** To be very simplistic, we can choose life or death by choosing obedience or rebellion...faith or doubt...

Which do we choose?

He who follows his own ideas in opposition to the direction of his superiors needs no devil to tempt him, for he is a devil to himself.

~ St. John Climacus

Scripture Observation Understanding Love

Sirach 16

For mercy and wrath are with the Lord; he is mighty to forgive, and he pours out wrath.

Sirach 16:11b

Many times there seems to be two very entrenched camps when considering God. One side figures He is this great being in the sky just waiting for us to mess up so He can yell a divine "Gottcha!" The other side figures He is chill...whatever, as long as it is all good. Both sides are wrong.

Describe this paradox between God's mercy and His wrath.

The last judgment shall fill sinners with terror, but will be a source of joy and sweetness to the elect; for the Lord will then give praise to each one according to his works.

~ St. Alphonsus Maria de Liguori

Sirach 17

How great is the mercy of the Lord and his forgiveness for those who turn to him!

Sirach 17:29

When was the last time you turned to God and *allowed* Him to forgive you? If you are carrying around guilt, go to confession...and then be at peace, rest in His unfailing, merciful love.

How happy I am to see myself imperfect and be in need of God's mercy.

~ St Therese of the Child Jesus

Scripture Observation Understanding Love

Sirach 18

Do not follow your base desires, but restrain your appetites.

Sirach 18:30

Have you ever told your husband or best friend, "Don't let me _____!" Or, "If you see me start to _____, then _____." What if we asked our Guardian Angel to step in and restrain us from whatever we might do? I would think they would be more trustworthy and watchful than our husband or friend. They desire our eternal salvation, not just helping us control our earthly passions.

"When tempted, invoke your Angel. He is more eager to help you than you are to be helped! Ignore the devil and do not be afraid of him: He trembles and flees at the sight of your Guardian Angel.

~ St. John Bosco

Sirach 19

Never repeat a conversation and you will lose nothing at all.

Sirach 19:7

I remember the first time I read that passage. I was **shocked** there was a verse in the Bible that

- A) Cared about how I used my mouth
- B) Was so practical in its admonition.

That one verse encouraged me to find other verses in my Bible concerning my speech. I grabbed a green highlighter and started highlighting verse after verse concerning how I was to use my mouth. To me, the color green represented life and I wanted my words to myself and others to be life giving.

Choose a highlighter or pen color and each time you come to a verse about our words or our mouth, underline it, highlight it or make a note in a separate journal.

Beware of much speaking, for it banishes from the soul the holy thoughts and recollection with God.

~ St. Dorotheus

Scripture Observation Understanding Love

Sirach 20

There is one who keeps silent because he has no answer, while another keeps silent because he knows when to speak.

Sirach 20:6

Let's do a quick examen of our words today? Did we speak when we should have remained silent? Were we silent when we should have spoken?

He who has become aware of his sins has controlled his tongue, but a talkative person has not yet come to know himself as he should.

~ St. John Climacus

SCRIPTURE **O**BSERVATION **U**NDERSTANDING **L**OVE

Sirach 21

*Whoever keeps the law controls his thoughts,
and wisdom is the fulfilment of the fear of the Lord.*

Sirach 21:11

Consider the correlation between keeping the law and controlling our thoughts...controlling our thoughts and keeping the law...

The first end I propose in our daily work is to do the will of God; secondly, to do it in the manner he wills it; and thirdly to do it because it is his will.

~ St. Elizabeth Ann Seton

Scripture Observation Understanding Love

Sirach 22

O that a guard were set over my mouth, and a seal of prudence upon my lips, that it may keep me from falling, so that my tongue may not destroy me!

Sirach 22:27

Wow! The Book of Sirach is really taking us to task on our words! But in case you have been reading these verses considering how you have spoken to others, *I am challenging you to consider these verses in light of how you have spoken to yourself.* Sometimes we speak in a tone or way to ourselves we would never dream of speaking to someone else. Am I right? Or am I right?

"Wisdom enters through love, silence, and mortification. It is great wisdom to know how to be silent and to look at neither the remarks, nor the deeds, nor the lives of others.

~ St. John of the Cross

Scripture Observation Understanding Love

Sirach 23

A man accustomed to use insulting words will never become disciplined all his days.

Sirach 23:15

A long time ago I heard the phrase, "Hurt people, hurt people." Let's ask ourselves, "Do we use insulting words?" And I am not just asking about how we speak to or about others. *Let's examine how we speak to ourselves.* If we are in the habit of using insulting words with ourselves, we will use them with/for others. Oh, maybe not out loud, that would be rude! But what about those words that roll around our head about others?

Hmm, think about that for a minute.

No one heals himself by wounding another.

~ St. Ambrose

Sirach 24

Like the vine, I bud forth delights,
and my blossoms become glorious and abundant fruit.

Sirach 24:17

Dr. Taylor Marshall writes, "…the created maternal Lady Wisdom of the Old Testament is a type of the Immaculate Virgin Mary. This has been the unbroken conviction of the Catholic Church, and especially the teaching of the Doctors of the Church such as St. Bernard of Clairvaux and St. Alphonsus Liguori. I'd like to emphasize that Lady Wisdom is not Mary per se, but merely the type of the historical Mary."

So when we come to these hard to understand verses in Sirach, the ones that speak of "Wisdom" let's consider them in light of the Blessed Virgin Mary.

Never be afraid of loving the Blessed Virgin too much. You can never love her more than Jesus did.

~ St. Maximilian Kolbe

Scripture Observation Understanding Love

Sirach 25

My soul takes pleasure in three things, and they are beautiful in the sight of the Lord and of men: agreement between brothers, friendship between neighbors, and a wife and a husband who live in harmony.

Sirach 25:1

I looked up a few synonyms for agreement and harmony. I'm going to replace those two words with some of the synonyms I found.

...understanding among brothers

...consistency among brothers

...a wife and a husband who live with understanding

...a wife and husband who live consistently

Interesting how "consistently" and "understanding" came up both times. I bet that is a good indication we need to spend some time considering if we are living "consistently" and with "understanding."

One must see God in everyone.

~ St. Catherine Laboure

Scripture Observation Understanding Love

Sirach 26

A silent wife is a gift of the Lord, and there is nothing so precious as a disciplined soul.

Sirach 26:14

Some people may get hung up the "silent wife." Not me, I came to a complete stop at "...a disciplined soul." Back to my trusty Thesaurus.

Disciplined: calm, law abiding, manageable, nonviolent, quiet, restrained, tranquil, at peace

I see a common set of themes in the Book of Sirach. Flip back through this study and journal and write down the chapters where we've considered some of those synonyms.

She who is silent everywhere finds peace.

~ St. Teresa Margaret

Scripture Observation Understanding Love

Sirach 27

If a man is not steadfast and zealous in the fear of the Lord, his house will be quickly overthrown.

Sirach 27:3

I do not know about you, but "steadfast" and "zealous" trip me up all the time. Well, maybe not so much zealous. I can get pretty zealous when it comes to Pinning a new color coded home management system or 50 Pins of just the right shade of blue cabinets! It is the steadfast part, the follow through that gets me. I lack the virtue of fortitude—"courage in pain or adversity." Yep, as soon as the going gets tough...I get going.

Name one area of your life where you could use a divine dose of fortitude. Write down one thing...**just one**...to add a little sticktoittiveness in that area. And do not forget to ask God to help you...and your Guardian Angel...and your patron saint.

To begin is for everyone. To persevere is for saints.

~ St. Josemaria Escriva

Scripture Observation Understanding Love

Sirach 28

The blow of a whip raises a welt, but a blow of the tongue crushes the bones.

Sirach 28:17

One of the synonyms for welt is "wound." Have you been wounded by someone's words? *Has that someone been you?* Examine how you have spoken to and about yourself today. Was it bone crushing?

You may need a dose of Ephesians 2:10...**I am God's masterpiece.**

Say that to yourself, in front of a mirror, three times a day, until...*until you believe it.*

No passion is worse than an uncontrolled tongue, because it is the mother of all the passions.

~ St. Agathon

Scripture Observation Understanding Love

Sirach 29

Be content with little or much.

Sirach 29:23

Contentment could be considered being satisfied with the life we live now. Here is a hard truth; if we cannot get to a place of contentment *where we are right now*, adding more or less...bigger or smaller, here or there, will not make us content. It will only shift our focus of discontent. That is why the author states "little *or* much."

No duty is more urgent than that of returning thanks.

~ St. Ambrose

Scripture Observation Understanding Love

Sirach 30

Good things poured out upon a mouth that is closed are like offerings of food placed upon a grave.

Sirach 30:18

This is a pretty funny analogy. Food on a grave? See, food is for nourishment (and pleasure). But the dead cannot eat for nourishment (or pleasure). So the food on the grave goes to waste.

Good things poured out on a closed mouth…a mouth shut to thanksgiving…is just as much a waste, as food on a grave.

The secret of happiness is to live moment by moment and to thank God for what He is sending us every day in His goodness.

~ St. Gianna Beretta Molla

*S*CRIPTURE *O*BSERVATION *U*NDERSTANDING *L*OVE

Sirach 31

Judge your neighbor's feelings by your own, and in every matter be thoughtful.

Sirach 31:15

How many times have we been offended by our neighbor's words or actions because we have assumed the worst intention behind those words or actions? I wonder why we would assume the worst? According this scripture, we should judge our neighbor's feelings by our own...*is that what we did, and we offended ourselves?!* Did we judge them according to our own feelings? Is that where the offense came from? Ourselves?

"What is the mark of love for your neighbor? Not to seek what is for your own benefit, but what is for the benefit of the one loved, both in body and in soul.

~ St. Basil the Great

Scripture Observation Understanding Love

Sirach 32

Do nothing without deliberation; and when you have acted, do not regret it.

Sirach 32:19

A little forethought, a little attention, a little carefulness can really go a long way to save us from sin, embarrassment, regret, sorrow...you name it.

I had a priest one time tell me if his sister had time, she would not make a decision for *30 days*. If she had the time to consider things that long, she felt 30 days allowed her mind to go through all necessary scenarios and her body to go through all its hormones! Then she could make a well-considered decision. We may not have 30 days, but maybe 30 minutes?

Go forth in peace, for you have followed the good road. Go forth without fear, for he who created you has made you holy, has always protected you, and loves you as a mother. Blessed be you, my God, for having created me.

~ St. Clare of Assisi

Scripture Observation Understanding Love

Sirach 33

Do not act immoderately toward anybody, and do nothing without discretion.

Sirach 33:29

The easiest way I can understand this verse is to break it down very simply. A synonym for immoderately is excessively. I am not to act excessively toward anybody—excessively happy, excessively sad, excessively talkative, excessively silent...

Let us go forward in peace, our eyes upon heaven, the only one goal of our labors.

~ St. Therese of Lisieux

Scripture Observation Understanding Love

Sirach 34

*He who fears the Lord will not be timid,
nor play the coward, for he is his hope.*

Sirach 34:14

Being a Christian woman is not for the weak of heart! We can and should be bold in our faith because our hope is in Christ. Let me assure you though, *bold does not equal brash.* No one likes a brash and brazen woman. No, our bold faith is brave, courageous and heroic. Choose a brave, courageous or heroic female saint to learn more about. For example: St. Joan of Arc, St. Maria Goretti or St. Clare of Assisi.

If you are what you should be, you will set the whole world ablaze!

~ St. Catherine of Sienna

Scripture Observation Understanding Love

Sirach 35

*Give to the Most High as he has given,
and as generously as your hand has found.*

Sirach 35:10

Can I just get this out there? I used to feel like my family took me for granted. I mean, how did they think their socks got clean…or even to the laundry for that matter? And the food in the pantry, well, it did not walk in there by itself. Guess who I was too busy serving? It was not them and it sure was not God. I was serving myself and my feelings. And that "taken for granted" feeling, it was not from the justice of God…it was from the pit of hell. The enemy was trying to stir up a big 'ol pot of discontent with my family, my home, my life, my entire vocation!

Can you image feeling like God was taking advantage of us when we did something for Him? Of course not! And that is what had to change. I had to start viewing my daily service *as a gift to Him* by serving my family—His beloved children. Does the enemy still try to mess with my head and heart in this area? You bettcha! I have to quickly recognize it as an attack, confess my selfishness and focus on serving God through my family.

Give something, however small, to the one in need. For it is not small to one who has nothing. Neither is it small to God, if we have given what we could.

~ St. Gregory Nazianzen

Sirach 36

*If kindness and humility mark her speech,
her husband is not like other men.*

Sirach 36:23

I can think of few things more uncomfortable than hearing a wife nag, belittle or just flat out insult her husband in front of others. Nobody wants to see the husband verbally correct or fight back...but nobody wants to see him sit there and take it either.

If you do this to your husband...**stop it right now.**

If you want your husband to be like no other man...treat him like no other man.

If you want your husband to treat you like no other woman...do not act like other women.

Teach us to give and not count the cost.

~ St. Ignatius de Loyola

Scripture Observation Understanding Love

Sirach 37

And besides all this pray to the Most High that he may direct your way in truth.

Sirach 37:15

This verse contains something I have not ever done...prayed to be directed in the Lord's truth. This verse is a reminder to me to pray about all things and before all things...and ask for His truth. I do not want to end up like Pontius Pilate asking "What is truth?" So I need to start praying now, *"Lord, show me Your truth."*

Grant me, O Lord my God, a mind to know you, a heart to seek you, wisdom to find you, conduct pleasing to you, faithful perseverance in waiting for you, and a hope of finally embracing you.

~ St. Thomas Aquinas

SCRIPTURE **O**BSERVATION **U**NDERSTANDING **L**OVE

Sirach 38

Do not give your heart to sorrow; drive it away, remembering the end of life.

Sirach 38:20

I would think remembering the end of life would bring sorrow? That is my earthly thinking rearing its ugly head! Putting my eternity thinking cap on makes me think of the scripture about sorrow lasting for a moment but joy coming in the morning.

This life contains the sorrow, sin, hurt, and ugliness. Eternity with God contains joy and peace. *So sorrowful thinking is earthly thinking.* And when it starts to creep in my heart and mind, I need to shift my focus to thoughts of the end of my life and eternity with God.

And if thoughts of eternity fill me with sorrow, I need to examine my conscience and see if there is some sin to confess that is clouding my visions of eternity.

The faith of those who live their faith is a serene faith. What you long for will be given you; what you love will be yours forever.

~ St. Leo the Great

Scripture Observation Understanding Love

Sirach 39

*The works of the Lord are all good,
and he will supply every need in its hour.*

Sirach 39:33

This would be a lovely verse to memorize and even repeat to a struggling friend, "The works of the Lord are all good." I can almost hear the birds chirping and the angels singing as we gush about how God will supply every need in its hour.

Come on, we are not fooling anyone. The last three words, we could totally do without them..."in its hour." Really, "In its hour!" Well! what if *its hour* does not line up with *my hour?!?* How sing-songy am I then? More like rolling around in agony asking "Whhyyyyy... Whhhheeeennnnnn..."

Let's really take this verse to heart. The whole, entire verse. I stand by my original sentence, "This would be a lovely verse to memorize and even repeat to a struggling friend," especially ourselves.

"Who except God can give you peace? Has the world ever been able to satisfy the heart?

~ St. Gerard Majella

Scripture Observation Understanding Love

Sirach 40

A friend or a companion never meets one amiss, but a wife with her husband is better than both

Sirach 40:23

Another translation on this verse is, "You can't go wrong with a good friend or neighbor, but an intelligent wife is better than either." So what is an intelligent wife? A couple of years ago at The Littlest Way, I wrote about an intelligent wife based on Sirach 25:8 I looked up 'intelligent' in the Thesaurus. Some of the synonyms were: creative, original, rational, all there, and ready. It was an interesting study on being an intelligent wife.

I am sure you have probably asked yourself before if you were a "good wife." Have you ever asked yourself if you are an intelligent wife?

If a marriage is to preserve its initial charm and beauty, both husband and wife should try to renew their love day after day, and that is done through sacrifice, with smiles and also with ingenuity.

~ St. Josemaria Escriva

Scripture Observation Understanding Love

Sirach 41

The days of a good life are numbered, but a good name endures forever.

Sirach 41:13

What are we doing? What are we making? I do not mean right now or what is for dinner. I mean what is the legacy we are building. Yes, you did know day by day we are building a legacy right? No, I am not talking about the article you wrote for a national magazine or leading the parish fundraiser or work outside the home. I am talking about the work you do in your home...what is the legacy you are building there?

When my mother in law died, the funeral director remarked he could not remember a longer procession line to the cemetery. My mother in law was a homemaker, in the literal sense. She made her home and it attracted others to it...to her. She loved...she loved well and long and just because. No one had to earn it, she just gave it.

I want a legacy of love...love for God and love for souls. I want a legacy that will outlast me here on earth and one I can take with me to Heaven.

In the evening of life, we will be judged on love alone.

~ St. John of the Cross

Scripture Observation Understanding Love

Sirach 42

Better is the wickedness of a man than a woman who does good; it is woman who brings shame and disgrace.

Sirach 42:14

What?!?!

"That is, there is, commonly speaking, less danger to be apprehended to the soul from the churlishness, or injuries we receive from men, than from the flattering favours and familiarity of women." (Challoner)

Is this true? Have you ever experienced "flattering favors?" Have you ever been the false flatterer?

Be gentle to all and stern with yourself.

~ St. Teresa of Avila

SCRIPTURE OBSERVATION UNDERSTANDING LOVE

Sirach 43

When you praise the Lord, exalt him as much as you can; for he will surpass even that. When you exalt him, put forth all your strength, and do not grow weary, for you cannot praise him enough.

Sirach 43:30

Did you pay attention to a few words or phrases in the passage?

"…as much as you can…"
"…he will surpass…"
"…all your strength…"
"…do not grow weary…"
"…you cannot praise him enough…"

Those are some pretty specific phrases and precise words.

Nothing is far from God.

~ St. Monica

Scripture Observation Understanding Love

Sirach 44

*Enoch pleased the Lord, and was taken up;
he was an example of repentance to all generations.*

Sirach 44:16

This verse begs the question, "What are we an example of to our family and friends? Strangers on the street or in the grocery store?" Are we an example of repentence? Love? Mercy?

Think of one relationship or situation right now and consider what example we are setting? Do we need to make some changes in the example we are setting?

Sanctify yourself and you will sanctify society.

~ St. Francis of Assisi

Scripture Observation Understanding Love

Sirach 45

He sanctified him through faithfulness and meekness; he chose him out of all mankind.

Sirach 45:4

This verse refers to Moses. In the New Jerusalem translation it states, "For his loyalty and gentleness he sanctified him, choosing him alone out of all human beings." But there is more. In verse 5, "...he allowed him to hear his voice and led him into the darkness..." This verse is explaining the characteristics of Moses—loyalty and gentleness or faithfulness and meekness—that led God to choose him, over and above anyone else. And in choosing Moses, God allowed him to hear His voice and He led Moses into the darkness to give him the commandments face to face.

Do we foster those virtues in our soul? Would God choose or has God chosen to lead us into the darkness *to hear His voice?*

Pain and suffering have come into your life, but remember pain, sorrow, suffering are but the kiss of Jesus - a sign that you have come so close to Him that He can kiss you.

~ Blessed Mother Teresa

Sirach 46

He (Joshua) called upon the Most High, the Mighty One, when enemies pressed him on every side,

Sirach 46:5

I would love to tell you how when I feel pressed on every side, I call upon the Most High. That would be a great story...not necessarily true, but a good story right?

So how do you handle feeling pressed on all sides from the enemy...or the toddler, the in-laws, the snarky momma on Facebook, the picture perfect PTA president, the seemingly irresponsible driver, the...well, you get the point.

Many cry to God, but not with the voice of the soul, but with the voice of the body; only the cry of the heart, of the soul, reaches God.

~ St. Augustine

SCRIPTURE OBSERVATION UNDERSTANDING LOVE

Sirach 47

In all that he did he gave thanks to the Holy One, the Most High, with ascriptions of glory; he sang praise with all his heart, and he loved his Maker.

Sirach 47:8

This passage, wow!   Take this passage and personalize it.

In all that **I** do, **I** give thanks to the Holy One, the Most High, with ascriptions (acknowledgement, credit, recognition) of glory, **I** sing praise with all **my** heart, and **I** love **my** maker.

Now, write your personalized version:

Remember the past with gratitude. Live the present with enthusiasm. Look forward to the future with confidence.

~ St. Pope John Paul II

Scripture Observation Understanding Love

Sirach 48

But they called upon the Lord who is merciful, spreading forth their hands toward him; and the Holy One quickly heard them from heaven, and delivered them by the hand of Isaiah.

Sirach 48:20

Sometimes, does it seem like God does not answer us? Not quickly...not slowly...not at all. I wonder, in those times, have we "called upon the Lord who is merciful?" Or have we wallowed, worried and wasted our time instead? Are we tossing limp prayers up to heaven like limp spaghetti...hoping they will stick?

It is our part to seek, His to grant what we ask; ours to make a beginning, His to bring it to completion; ours to offer what we can, His to finish what we cannot.

~ St. Jerome

Scripture Observation Understanding Love

Sirach 49

He set his heart upon the Lord;
in the days of wicked men he strengthened godliness.

Sirach 49:3

This verse refers to Josiah, a King of Judah. It states, "...he strengthened godliness." I would expect it to say, "He was strengthened in godliness."

In the New Jerusalem translations it states, "...he set his heart on the Lord, in godless times he upheld the cause of religion."

Let's be the Josiah's of this generation...or at least our circle of friends. Let's set our hearts on God and encourage those who do as well.

For Jesus Christ I am prepared to suffer still more.

~ St. Maximilian Kolbe

Scripture Observation Understanding Love

Sirach 50

And now bless the God of all, who in every way does great things; who exalts our days from birth, and deals with us according to his mercy.

Sirach 50:22

One of the things I most appreciate about God is His mercy towards me. I know there are people I need to be more merciful with, how about you? Let's write the name of one of those people down and ask God to help us be merciful to them. Ask for *His eyes* to see them and *His heart* to love them.

Mercy imitates God and disappoints Satan.

~ St. John Chrysostom

Scripture Observation Understanding Love

Sirach 51

The Lord gave me a tongue as my reward, and I will praise him with it.

Sirach 51:22

I pray one of the lessons we have learned is how powerful our words are. This verse makes it very clear our tongue is a gift, a reward from the Lord. Please, let's use this gift to praise God...everyday...all day.

Make sure that your thanksgiving comes pouring out from your heart every day.

~ St. Josemaria Escriva

If It Were Not for You All...

For an introverted heart, I am surrounded by lovely souls.

I know for a fact the good Lord has a sense of humor! He abundantly blessed this quiet momma with seven noisy children. They keep me moving, humble me, bring me to my knees, and make me laugh, think and cry. They know how to break me wide open and that's a good thing, making more room for love.

I know for a fact the good Lord watches over me. He blessed me with a strong and steady husband. Chris smooths my rough edges, calms my anxious mind and shows me the kind of unconditional love God has for me.

I know for a fact the good Lord encourages me. He gives me the example and friendship of women, in real life and online, who get up every morning and try again. Y'all encourage me!

I know for a fact the good Lord loves me. He gave me His only Son, Who laid down His life for me...there is no greater love than that.

Made in the USA
Lexington, KY
08 November 2017